Keep Your Word

To get the complete **Idioms for Inclusivity** experience, this book can be purchased alongside four others as a set, *Idioms for Inclusivity: Fostering Belonging with Language*, **978-1-032-28635-8**.

Informed by sociolinguistic research, yet written accessibly, *Keep Your Word* challenges readers to investigate the act of promising as it relates to both language-use and inclusivity.

This engaging and delightfully illustrated book invites students to engage with concepts such as:

- the cultural meaning of the idiom "keep your word"

- Speech Acts and Felicity Conditions, two frameworks that linguists use to research and understand promises

- why the expectation to "keep your word" can make someone feel excluded

- how understanding the way language works can help us learn to be more inclusive

Featuring practical inclusivity tips related to promises, this enriching curriculum supplement can be used in a Language Arts setting to learn about figurative language; in a Social Studies setting to discuss diversity, equity, inclusion, and belonging; or as an introduction to linguistics for students aged 7–14.

Samantha Beaver is a workplace communications analyst and linguist. She has been involved in language research and teaching/training since 2013. She is currently CEO and Founder of Memra Language Services.

KEEP YOUR WORD

DISCUSSING PROMISES

SAMANTHA BEAVER

ILLUSTRATED BY
MELISSA LEE JOHNSON

Routledge
Taylor & Francis Group
NEW YORK AND LONDON

Designed cover image: Illustrated by Melissa Lee Johnson

First published 2023
by Routledge
605 Third Avenue, New York, NY 10158

and by Routledge
4 Park Square, Milton Park, Abingdon, Oxon, OX14 4RN

Routledge is an imprint of the Taylor & Francis Group, an informa business

Illustrated by Melissa Lee Johnson

ISBN: 978-1-032-29340-0 (hbk)
ISBN: 978-1-032-28637-2 (pbk)
ISBN: 978-1-003-30113-4 (ebk)

DOI: 10.4324/9781003301134

Typeset in Futura
by Deanta Global Publishing Services, Chennai, India

Contents

CHAPTER 1

About This Book

DOI: 10.4324/9781003301134-1

The Language Idioms for Inclusivity series is a collection of short, illustrated books for ages 7–14 that use common language idioms to explore concepts related to inclusivity. This exploration is informed by sociolinguistic and pragmatic research but is written in a readable format, wherein the author poses probing questions to the reader and guides them through linguistic analysis by suggesting possible answers.

This series introduces children to key concepts in linguistics and gives them (and their parents or instructors) a new, language-oriented framework to use when discussing issues of inclusion.

Keep Your Word: Discussing Promises is the second installment in the Language Idioms for Inclusivity series. In this book, the author challenges readers to investigate promises as they relate to both language-use and inclusivity. The author does this by (1) explaining the cultural meaning of the idiom, "keep your word"; (2) introducing Speech Acts and Felicity Conditions, two frameworks that linguists use to research and understand promises; and (3) explaining why the expectation to "keep your word" could make someone feel excluded. The book ends with a description of how understanding the way language works can help us be more inclusive and practical language tips to integrate learning into daily conversations.

As a supplement to traditional curriculum, this book can be used in a Language Arts setting to learn about figurative language; in a Social Studies setting to discuss diversity, equity, inclusion, and belonging; or as an introduction to linguistics, a college-level subject that is not typically offered to K–12 students.

CHAPTER 2

How to Use This Book in Your Teaching Practice

DOI: 10.4324/9781003301134-2

In whichever context you choose to read this book, here are some suggestions for integrating it into teaching.

1. *Always Aloud, Always Together*

When using it in the classroom or at home, read this book aloud and with your 7–14-year-old. The concepts in this book are new and abstract, but the tone of the book speaks to a middle-school audience. Likewise, the illustrations are meant to be seen and enhance the intended learning. Experiencing this book together connects the teacher and learner in a way that promotes questioning, critical thinking, and side-by-side learning. These ideas might be just as new for you as they are for your students! What a wonderful opportunity to learn together.

2. *Use Yourself as an Example*

Familiarize yourself with the book before using it in the classroom. After reading through the concepts and examples, try to think of some real language examples from conversations that you've experienced that reflect the intended learning. Be vulnerable and tell your students about a time when you made a mistake or failed to keep a promise. By using real examples from your real life, you will extend the feeling that this is a mutual learning experience – and an ongoing one! We are never done learning how to communicate with one another. Your students will feel respected and honored that you are placing yourself in the position of "learner" with them.

3. *Reflect in Discussion*

The intended learnings in this book can be practiced and integrated well into discussion-based activities. Some ideas:

- Create examples of everyday promises ("study for math test," "screens off by eight," etc) and write them on a stack of note cards. Also on note cards, describe different types of people ("your mom," "a 15-year-old hispanic boy," etc). In groups, ask students to pull out one promise card and one person card. Have them discuss whether they think that person would be able to make/keep that promise. Would an adult believe them? Would a kid believe them? Why or why not?

- Using the Practical Language Tips at the back of this book, ask students to practice having clarifying and inclusive conversations. Give them topics or scenarios to discuss as they practice.

4. *Reflect in Writing*

The intended lessons in this book can be practiced and integrated well into writing-based activities. Some ideas:

- Have students create a Belonging Journal. Give writing prompts and allow for 10–15 minutes of writing time for self-reflection. Prompts should offer a range of writing-types, including but not limited to:

  - Brainstorming ("Word Is Bond" is a phrase that originated from hip-hop music and is common in African-American English. Brainstorm some guesses about what this phrase means and write them down. Do you think this phrase would mean something different if a Black person said it than if a White person did? Why or why not?).

  - Self-reflection (write about a time when an adult didn't trust you to follow through with what you said you would do. How did that feel? Did you end up following though anyway, or did you fail because you knew they expected you to fail?).

  - Creative writing (create a character who no one ever believes or trusts – especially when that character tries to make a promise. Describe what they are like and how they live. Write a dialog between your character and one other person who refuses to trust them.).

- Have students write an editorial essay. Ask them to share their opinion on an idea or topic presented in this book. Do they agree? Do they disagree? What about their cultural and family background influences what they think? Do they think their friends would agree with them? Their grandparents? Why or why not?

5. *Reflect in Hypothetical Thinking*

The intended learnings in this book can be practiced and integrated well into critical-thinking activities (which can be realized in writing or in discussion). Some ideas:

- Challenge students to respond to a hypothetical "promising-conversation" between two people that has three possible outcomes. Ask them to identify what would need to happen for each of the outcomes to occur. Ask them to choose which scenario is most likely to happen in real life (or at their school). Ask them why and whether that is a good or bad thing.

- Ask students to create a hypothetical world (or school) where everyone is culturally the same. In this world, is it easier to trust people to do what they say they are going to do? Are humans still biased in this world? Or are they always reasonable?

Thank you for choosing this book and engaging with these ideas. For more ideas about or support in using linguistics and inclusivity in the classroom, visit www.mem ralanguageservices.com.

CHAPTER 3

Glossary

DOI: 10.4324/9781003301134-3

belief – accepting that something is true, often regardless of whether evidence supports it as true or not.

bias – preferring or believing one thing or reality over another reality or thing – in a way that is unfair.

clausal phrases – a phrase that has both a subject and a predicate but is not a sentence.

felicity conditions – language rules that tell the listener whether a speech act is effective or not.

hypothesis – an educated guess that can be tested using the scientific method.

idiomatic expression – a well-known phrase that carries a well-known cultural meaning.

illocutionary act – a speech act where the action you are taking is the language you are using.

linguists – language scientists; people who study how human language works, both in the brain and out in the world.

past tense – the grammatical tense that places actions and situations into the past. The past tense usually places special markers on the end of verbs.

plural pronoun – a word or group of words that can be substituted for a noun or noun phrase referring to more than one person, place, or thing.

promise – getting someone to believe that you are going to do what you said you were going to do.

reasoning – when you think and understand things by way of their cause, explanation, or evidence.

speech act – a linguistic idea that describes when a sentence doesn't just tell you something, but actually does something.

CHAPTER 4

The Idiom

DOI: 10.4324/9781003301134-4

What does it mean when someone says, "KEEP YOUR WORD"?

KEEP YOUR WORD is a phrase you've probably heard your parents or teachers use. Most of the time, this phrase is used like this: "You need to keep your word!" or "You didn't keep your word!"

Maybe you heard this phrase when you told your mom you would clean your room before going outside to play with your friends ... but then you didn't actually clean your room.

Or maybe when you told your teacher you would turn in a make-up assignment on Friday ... but then you didn't turn it in.

When someone says, "KEEP YOUR WORD," they are using an **idiomatic expression**. An idiomatic expression is a well-known phrase that carries a well-known cultural meaning. The words in an idiomatic expression don't always make sense if you think about them outside of your cultural context.

For example, when someone says, "He has a short fuse," you know that they mean "he gets angry quickly" – even though the actual words "short fuse" don't mean that on their own. There are lots of idioms in every language and idioms can tell us a lot about the people who speak that language.

In this book, we are talking about the idiom, "KEEP YOUR WORD!". When someone says KEEP YOUR WORD, what they really mean is "do what you say you are going to do."

"do what you say you are going to do."

Doing what you say you are going to do can also be thought of as **following through on a promise**.

Promising can be tricky: sometimes we mean what we say, and sometimes we don't. Why and when do humans expect other humans to do what they say they are going to do? How do you know when someone is making a promise?

CHAPTER 5

The Linguistic Theory

DOI: 10.4324/9781003301134-5

Language experts, called **linguists**, have thought about this question a lot. Many of them have come up with guesses, also called **hypotheses**, that explain how humans make promises. Most of these guesses involve one key idea called the

Speech Act

A Speech Act is the part of a sentence that doesn't just TELL us something, but actually DOES something. For example, when your parents first named you, at some point they said: "His name is Otto." That sentence was the ACTION that gave you your name.

We use Speech Acts to

REQUEST (getting someone to give you something): *Pass the salt!*

SCARE (making someone feel afraid): *On a dark and stormy night …*

INSULT (getting someone to feel offended): *Your feet stink!*

AMUSE (getting someone to laugh): *Knock, Knock! Who's there? Orange. Orange who? Orange you glad I didn't say banana?*

And of course,

PROMISE (getting someone to believe that you are going to do what you said you were going to do): *I will call you when I'm on my way home!*

These types of Speech Acts are called **Illocutionary Acts**. Illocution means speaking or writing IS the action you are doing.

In order for a promise to be a successful illocutionary act, the person making the promise has to KEEP THEIR WORD.

So, how do you know when someone will KEEP THEIR WORD? How can you tell the difference between when someone means what they say and when they don't mean what they say?

There are language rules, called **Felicity Conditions**, about what makes a promise real. Imagine that your friend from school says this:

I promise that I will bring you a piece of bubble gum tomorrow.

There are six rules that tell you (the listener) whether this is a real promise or not:

Rule 1 SINCERE SPEAKER – your friend needs *to intend* to actually bring you bubble gum tomorrow.

Rule 2 UNDERSTANDING LISTENER – you need to *understand* that your friend is making a promise.

Rule 3 FUTURE ACTION – the bubble gum needs to be given to you in the future.

Rule 4 ABLE SPEAKER – your friend needs to actually *be able* to bring the bubble gum to you tomorrow.

Rule 5 SOMETHING SPECIAL – bringing you bubble gum needs to be *something special* – something that your friend doesn't always do everyday.

Rule 6 LISTENER BENEFITS – bubble gum needs to be something that you *like and want*.

When you hear a promise, your brain automatically thinks about all of these rules in order to decide whether the promise is successful as an illocutionary act – or to decide whether the speaker will KEEP THEIR WORD. If one of the rules is not followed, then the promise might not be a successful illocution.

Understanding these rules helps us understand why the expectation for someone to KEEP THEIR WORD can be **biased**.

When something is biased, it means it is taking one reality into account (or preferring one thing) over another reality or thing – without a good reason to do so.

Two rules about promising are especially likely to be **biased**: (1) the SINCERE SPEAKER rule and (4) the ABLE SPEAKER rule.

When our brains are trying to decide whether a speaker is SINCERE or ABLE, what we are really doing is determining whether we are going to **believe** what the speaker is saying. To do this, we take some evidence into account, like what we have seen that speaker do in the past, but we also let cultural bias contribute to our decision.

For example, if your mom rarely picks you up from school on time, you might not BELIEVE her when she says she will come and get you at 4:00. This conclusion is justified based on your previous experiences.

On the other hand, imagine your parents hire a babysitter to watch you and your siblings for the night. When they hire a girl babysitter, maybe they leave behind only emergency phone numbers and a frozen pizza; but when they hire a boy babysitter, maybe they leave a whole page of detailed instructions, including how to use the oven and where to find the toddler's pajamas. Your parents don't BELIEVE that the boy babysitter knows how to take care of you and your siblings (even if they would never say that out loud). This is a **biased** conclusion that is probably not based on their experiences, but rather the cultural idea that girls are better caregivers than boys.

Every human brain is sometimes **reasonable** and sometimes biased.

When it comes to promising, humans usually expect people they are biased against to KEEP THEIR WORD, while at the same time not truly believing that those same people are actually capable of making and following through on a real promise.

And because our brains are more likely to be biased against people who are different from us, this problem can put marginalized groups in impossible situations.

They are expected to keep their word, but are not trusted or believed to do so.

CHAPTER 6

The Inclusive Solution

DOI: 10.4324/9781003301134-6

Promising-bias can create miscommunications, but it doesn't have to be this way. Here are three examples of how speech acts can make our understanding of promises more inclusive:

- **In order for a promise to be a successful illocution, the speaker has to be SINCERE.**

  You used to think Roman was acting crazy when he would get angry if you didn't come back outside after dinner to skate.

  Now you can understand that Roman thinks you are making a promise when you say: *"I'll come back out after dinner!,"* when actually, your intention for that sentence is not to promise but to express hope (*"I hope I can come back out after dinner!"* or *"I'll come back out after dinner … if I can!"*). Roman gets mad because it seems like you are being insincere. Now, because you understand how speech acts work, you can explain that you ARE being SINCERE: you are sincere *in hoping* that you can come back out, but are not making a sincere promise.

- **In order for a promise to be a successful illocution, the speaker has to be ABLE to do what they said they would do.**

  You used to think that because Lani's family doesn't own a car, that Lani probably wouldn't follow through when she said she would meet you at the library every Wednesday afternoon to work on your school project, so you tried to do most of it yourself at home.

  Now you can understand that your conclusion about Lani was biased. Because Lani is different from you (her family doesn't own a car, and your family does), you assumed that she was less ABLE to make a successful illocutionary promise. Now, because you understand how speech acts work, you can explain to yourself that you didn't have a good reason to mistrust Lani, and you can try to believe her promise next time.

- **In order for a promise to be a successful illocution, the listener has to UNDERSTAND that they are being promised something.**

  You used to think your Mexican-American friend, Gabriel, was blowing you off when he biked to school even though you told him you would pick him up.

  Now you can understand that Gabriel didn't interpret your sentence "I can pick you up tomorrow!" as a promise. Instead, your sentence had the illocutionary effect of expressing only what you were *able* to do, but not what you were *going to* do. Now, because you understand how speech acts work, you can explain why Gabriel isn't actually blowing you off, and make a more explicit promise next time.

Learning about Speech Acts and their Felicity Conditions gives us a new way to understand how people make promises with words – and how people who are different from us can experience unfair expectations to KEEP THEIR WORD.

When we focus on language, we can discover a new way to solve an old problem.

CHAPTER 7

Practical Language Tips

DOI: 10.4324/9781003301134-7

Try these language strategies in conversation, like when you need someone to make or keep a promise but you are having a hard time believing that they will follow through.

1. *Don't Talk → Ask Yourself Why: Reason or Bias?*

When you notice that you distrust someone's promise to you, ask yourself whether the distrust is based on real experiences that you've had with that person, or whether it's based on cultural bias that has nothing to do with that specific person. Try asking yourself these questions:

- Has this person failed to follow through on a promise before? What caused them to fail?

- Is this person from an underrepresented group? Do I secretly think they are incapable of keeping a promise because they belong to that group?

- Why do I need this person to promise me something? Is there a different way to get what I need or want?

2. *Ask for Commitment in a New Way*

The language we use to get other people to make promises can be exclusionary, especially when we consider bias. But there are lots of ways to ask someone to make a commitment; try something new!

- Trust Positive Actions and Encourage Repetition

    o *Hey, Maya **helped us win** that basketball game; she should be on our team again tomorrow.*

    - Describing positive things that someone did in the **past-tense** like, "helped us win," forms an argument that they might do that same positive thing again.

    o *I saw how you made corrections on last week's assignment; **that is a great way** to seriously boost your grade!*

    - Using **causal phrases** like, "that is a great way to ..." or "since doing X, Y has gotten better" draw attention to the impact that a positive action can have, which reinforces the value of those actions in the first place.

- Give More than One Way to Commit Successfully

  - *Are you bringing bubble gum tomorrow or **should we** go to the gas station after school to get more?*

    - Using the **plural pronoun "we"** gives the promiser the option of sharing responsibility with YOU for the outcome of the promise, instead of taking on the full responsibility themselves.

  - ***Can you play on our team again?** If you want to be our fifth player, you can have the spot, otherwise you can play as our sixth and sub in.*

    - Using a **question-answer format**, where you ask a question about ability while also providing the answer(s) you hope to receive, gives the promiser pre-prepared language to use when they make their commitment to you.

Bibliography

Bibliography

Ahearn, L. M. (2021). *Living language: An introduction to linguistic anthropology.* John Wiley & Sons.

Archer, D., Aijmer, K., & Wichmann, A. (2013). *Pragmatics: An advanced resource book for students.* Routledge.

Austin, J. L. (1962). *How to do things with words.* Harvard.

Searle, J. R., & Searle, J. R. (1969). *Speech acts: An essay in the philosophy of language* (Vol. 626). Cambridge University Press.

Meet the Author and Illustrator

Meet the Author

Samantha Beaver is a linguist. She got her Master's Degree in Applied English Linguistics from the University of Wisconsin-Madison. Sociolinguistics, Pragmatics, and Conversation Analysis are her areas of linguistic expertise, and her favorite topics to explore are language equity, language and gender, language learning, language and people management, and language and power. When she's not doing linguistic work for other people, she is at home fostering the language development of her two sons, Simon and Louis. You can learn more about Samantha's work at www.memralanguageservices.com.

Meet the Illustrator

Melissa Lee Johnson is an award-winning artist, illustrator, and graphic designer. She graduated with a Bachelor of Fine Arts in Integrated Studio Arts from the Milwaukee Institute of Art and Design and got her start illustrating for an alternative newspaper. In 2020 she received the Communication Arts Illustration Annual Award of Excellence in Advertising. She currently works for Made By Things, a small animation studio based in Columbus, Ohio. When she's not drawing, she likes to hang with Bambi, Sparkle, and Trixie, her three rescue Chihuahuas. You can learn more about her at melissaleejohnsonart.com.

Samantha and Melissa became best friends when they were middle schoolers. Even back then, they often imagined teaming up to write and illustrate a book together someday. The content of this book is especially meaningful for them, because it wasn't always easy to remain friends and accept each other's differences and decisions as they grew into adults. A patient persistence has allowed them to hold fast to what now feels like sisterhood, and they hope that readers of this book learn that the best way to love someone who is different from you is to simply *keep trying*.